MW01601024

Promenade Sentimental

(A Collection of Poetry)

By: Carole Duquette

Written by: Carole Duquette

Cover Design: Jeremy Martin

Editorial: Carole Duquette

Author photo taken by: Angelique Martin

Copyright 2022 by: Carole Duquette

Published by Carole Duquette

ISBN: 9798800310177

All rights reserved. This book may not be reproduced in whole or in part without written permission from the publisher, except by a reviewer who may quote brief passages in review; nor may any part of this book be reproduced, stored in a retrieval system, or transmitted in any form or by any means, electronic, mechanical, photocopying, recording, or other, without written permission from the publisher.

Acknowledgments

Carole Duquette would like to thank her family and friends for their endless encouragement throughout the writing of her poetry work.

A special thanks to her Son Jeremy Martin for helping her to publish this book.

A special thank you to Polar Expression Publishing for supporting and encouraging her creativity as a Poet and for publishing four Poem's from her poetry work.

May you enjoy every poem written by Carole Duquette.

May it reach your heart and soul as it is the seed from which it was planted from.

May her poetry help you heal, find hope, and help you move forward along the journey of life.

May the sweetness, beauty and imagination of her poetry empower you to reach higher mountains.

Always remember you are an amazing person; you are strong and that no matter how bad a storm gets you can surpass it.

Always believe in yourself and follow the dreams that lie within your heart.

Table of Contents

Lean on

Throughout life you will find
Darkness can invade and leave you behind

At your lowest you will be

When your vessel sinks to sea

Afloat you will wonder

What came to save you from under

Had there been a miracle or not your time

Had you form power in your downtime

Life can certainly flicker one's light

Some in prayer will recite

Some will read a book to inspire

Some will reach to one they admire

Shadows let us down

Unless we are visible to be found

Turbulence can steer our hearts

An idea can create an art

When your world becomes somber

Lean on, one to nurture...

Callousness

Squeezing hard on my chest

Powerless to breath, I was a mess

Like an ant crushed in footpath

A sentimental fool, the aftermath

Pumped from my heart the beat had

Innermost, was a feeling so sad

The beautiful soul escaped from inside
There was no where for bruises to hide

Underneath the skin it started to peel

Nothing anymore that I could feel

As I took a breath of fresh air

The tears erupted, how dare

The falls had no time to be stopped

In labored breathing I was distraught

Pouring a coffee as I couldn't sleep

Feeling a void, an emptiness so deep

In the bathroom I discharged a bath

Immersed in water the ability lacked

Dragging my feet, I combed my hair

The pain inside I could no longer bare

Cried some more while sipping on coffee

In the interior of my core, it was empty

Sleep deprived and extinguished

An internal part was demolished

On my knees barely walking

In my head I still heard talking

Conjuncture of cruelty and Callousness

Against my heart it was helpless...

Hope can be found

In dark moments, hope can be lost

Emotions and feelings are tossed

Deep thoughts circulate and spread

An outcome, inside that bled

The soul was taken

Through a blind eye, forgotten

None of this was real

A wound that couldn't heal

The mind was without rest

The heart and soul against itself

Vulnerable enough to be crushed

The world was turning to dust

The strength had better come quicker

The mind was getting sicker

The lies were on fire

The truth was dug deeper

The greatest battles

Are with ourselves

A mind is a powerful weapon

That can leave you heartbroken

In dark moments, hope can be found

Emotions and feelings can turn around

Deep thoughts can make you stronger

An outcome that will bring you farther...

Unemotional Silence

Darkness fills the night with fear

Nothing anymore seems clear

Insomnia is a friend of mine

Seems were up all the time

I hear voices inside my head

Telling me what I should have said

My tongue was bitten by a snake

Evil doers are at stake

By choosing carefully my word

Will I leave my world unstirred?

If I shout it all out

Will I leave my world in doubt?

If my lips were not meant to move

Would a kiss be approved?

Whispering in his ears

This could calm my fears

Keeping my head above water

In silence I could lose her

If my body started shaking now

Would he hold me in his arms somehow?

If my innocence was taken over

Could his love make it better?

Veracity was a token

Solely I was broken

If explosions ignited in the night

Would he hold me tight

Lips, mouth and silence

A writer has been sentenced

In my newfound stillness

Feeling tireless

If my hope was running low

And my tears would overflow

Would he let me know...?

In silence I wait

To decide my faith ...

Empath Mystic

Deep inside her roots

Seeding delicately each fruit

An energy lifted her up

In her sweet, sweet shrub

Her garden was growing

A beautiful glow was shining

She found peace at her side

Until the negative would divide

A tug of war pulled her back

Her sentiment off track

Her warmth misunderstood

Her existence in another hood

No one could figure her symbol

Head strong and knowledgeable

Sugary and sweetened in her soul

Her heart was like gold

Always being real

With so much to feel

Different in her ways

A panel of judge nowadays

If she hid her beauty

Would one like her messy?

If she opened her heart

Would one tear her apart?

If she was a rare desert

Would one be worth her efforts?

If she was an Empath Mystic

Would one dare to sweep her off her feet?

Let's talk about Whoopee...

Hello! Do you hear me?

On my wall did you see?

Put your glasses, make it clearer

Oh Wait! My wall's gone further

Let me retrieve it from the mirror

Oh My! What a horror

Why did you ignore this page?

How do my words fill you with rage?

Wait I need to show you

What it's loose, my screw

Ouch! Your words are brutal

Why is everyone so cruel?

Hold on this will change your mind?

Don't you are about my kind?

Yes, I'm crying

You think I'm lying

Oh Wait! No one's there
Does anyone care?

Hey! What are you doing?

Really? Your caring

Woah! That's new

Is it true?

You love me

You don't even know me
You care for Humpty Dumpty have you gone crazy?

Oh! Really your on my side
Do you think we could override?

Oh! Wow I'm loving this
Can I add you to my list?

Friends are heavenly

Let's talk about Whoopee...

Castles in Spain

Wrapped inside her shell

Holding her pride, she fell

Suppressing emotions, she was sensible

Her numbness was inevitable

A loss grieved in silence

By her kind indulgence

In solitude for days on end

A love she had abandon

True colors had surfaced

Of one she had loved dearest

Onions peeled deepest in her soul

As she was no longer heart-whole

Unexpressed in her innermost feelings

Close- mouthed in her bearings

She was despondent in her awakening

Aspiring to save her being

Fantasy became part of her mind

Leaving her pain behind

Exalted delights in her vision

Longing for such compassion

Aroused in her introspections

Endless fairy tales to heal her emotions

As the time moved on

Her reality dawned

Forever would never be

As their souls came to see

Driving through the snow

Her eyes filled with sorrow

Would her heart love again?

Would there be a chance in?

Her illusions had perfected a man

Would she find him in her lifespan?

Amazing and sweet in her fabrication

A gentleman in her imagination

A lustrous mirage

A blissful Swedish massage

All of which were Castles in Spain

To love another for now she'd refrain...

Amity, Devotion, Togetherness

Why do we live in a world of dates?

A world that decides when we celebrate

Valentine's Day is for lovers - Is it really?

I beg to differ, it's for everyone truly

Yes, Valentine's Day should be all year

Everyday saying how we feel

Our world needs more love, not hate

We need to unite, not separate

One word can make you feel special

Valentine's Day to me is Superficial

A three-letter word I love you

Can be a lifeline for someone you knew

Don't wait for Valentine's Day

Show the world you care today

Be the change you want to see

Relieve hatred from the world, break free

United as one in love and harmony

With your heart make this world see

Today I vow to be the change

My heart is pure, nothing will change

I love all my friends and family

I love helping others in Unity

Message to the world I love U

I wish the very best for you

Amity, Devotion and Togetherness
The world needs your kindness...

Fulfill your prophecy

A beautiful mind inside her

A life force was stronger

She was lovely all around

Confident on solid ground

A chance encounter with a man

Asking her for her hand

An engagement of intimacy

She loved him profoundly

Creating a life together

In Matrimony forever

Unlucky in her shuffle

An illness left her puzzled

The ups and downs she contented

Never to fall she pretended

A war began in her perception

Catastrophic destruction

Knowing well about her consternation

Seeking answers in desperation

Pointless to reminisce of right or wrong

Here and now, she was dragging along

Formerly in seventh heaven

Presently in desolation

Time is a capsule that elapses

Internally there are messages

Alone in our undertaking

Matching up our awakening

A soul, mind and body

Became quite heavy

Take in consideration your fervor

Bear in mind what you stand for

When your world is somber

Explore your soul better

Release your Obscurity

Fulfill your prophecy

Memories Remain

When two worlds collide

She wants to hide

Dazed in a trance

A love had no chance

Remaining there for years

Now a river of broken tears

Covered in leashes

A core rip to pieces

A sprinkle of salt on her body

Her sentiment was heavy

Her skin had needles and pins

Numbness begins

Fearful, he controlled

Suffocating her soul

Self regarding his needs

Inside she bleeds

In harmony pretending

Over cycles repeating

Separating on their voyage Carrying heavy baggage

Nothing last forever

When he pulls her further

Nothing can mend the hearts

When two worlds fall apart

One last kiss goodbye

As their life passed them by

In Solidarity she found

The girl that had drowned

Memories will remain

Never to be the same...

Pie in the sky

A radiant woman was loss

A salad of love was toss

Compassionate and kind

His Ego was blind

Written on her heart

A story fell apart

Riding, the midnight train

Hoping, to pull through her pain

Hands covering her face

Her tears she could taste

A stranger approached her

Touching her shoulder

Leaning in to wipe her tears

His kindness was dear

He handled her gently

She felt pretty

As the train came to a stop

She was no longer distraught

A chance encounters

Made her world better

Connecting as one

A passion begun

Promenading on the lakeside

There fire was wide

Caressing every inch of her body

Her breath became heavy

Undressing her with his eyes

He became hypnotize

Wanting so badly each other

Cloud nine took over

Beyond anything they ever felt

Two hearts had melt

Smiling so widely

She wasn't ready

To leave her cage of thought

Where the magic wouldn't stop

Bringing her life higher

In her desire

Pie in the sky

Her life was passing her by

Mind's eye

Her vicarious emotions and pity

Were absent minded on High Society

Her mind became exhausted

In truth, life turned unexpected

Guarding her heart, against the storm

Unable to speak out, she was torn

Miles away she disappeared

In a fantasy world it was clear

Laying down on soft sand

A gentleman, held her hand

In his arms, holding her tight

His touch, felt so right

Resting on his chest

She only asked for one request

If I let you in my life

Would you cut me like a knife?

If I gave you all of me

Would you change, my identity

If I showed you what I need

Would you be absorbed in greed?

If I shared with you my dream,
Would you bury my only seed?

If I showed the world I cared

Would you be selfish, would you dare?

Gently he looked in her eyes

Feeling deeply all her cries

Placing his hands on her hips

Softly he kissed her lips

Feeling him inside her essence

He gave her his perception

If I promise to be all you want

Would you leave my heart in daunt?

If I treat you like a queen

Would you always come clean?

If I let you see my soul

Would you leave me in the cold?

Two broken spirits had met

Both carrying regret

She looked into his eyes

She promised to never lie

She frenched his lips of honey

She made him feel so sexy

He knew right then and there

He'd found a diamond that's rare

As she awoken from fantasy

She knew she wasn't happy

She needed to move on

There love had been far gone

Through her mind's eye

Nevermore to hear her cry...

Heavy heart

Burning bridges all around

Broken souls are falling down
Tortured in their minds

By evil humankind

Forty winks are disturbed

In a world so absurd

Painting murals on the wall

Innocent lives as they fall

Turned away by your blood

Powerless words of tongue

Pulling teeth as you're shun

The revolution has begun

Asleep, too blind to see

A world is no longer free

Finding strength in the unfamiliar

As the enemy creates a thriller

Higher grounds finding faith

Hoping the matrix to escape Tormented everyday

Dumbing down to find a way

A convoy drives in the night

Shining upon us a vivid light

Ours hearts are filled with joy

Still, we are paranoid

The dark days bled us good

Hardships we withstood

Democracy and fear

Our intentions they were clear

Freedom is our human right

To have our lives we will fight

Heavy heart filled a stream
We raised the flag against the regime...

A Taste so sweet

Passing time searching for the right quote
With a pen was just a stroke

Yearning for a beautiful life
I remained true to life

Even the darkest of days could not shatter
The pieces I was putting together

In all honesty
I trembled intensely

A river flooded in front of me
Through the tears I could see

Determined to rise above
The most broken of love

Reeling me in without power

I became so much stronger

Down the narrowed path

Seeing myself at last

In love, in tears, in life
Everyone pays a price

Fear can hold us there
Our hearts can break and tear

If you take one deep breath
If you look at your life in depth

You will see, a new beginning

A reason to keep on shining

Through the darkest of days
I saw my soul's rays

Found in the storm
I was transformed

A taste so sweet

I was swept off my feet ...

Unknown

Confusion took part

Crushing her heart

Words in silence

She was conscience

Nothing felt right

Blocking her light

Anxiety multiplied

In her room she cried

Only seeing his pain

Her world was to blame

Feeding her mind

Blocking her sunshine,
The darkness creeped in

Her head would spin

Unable to sleep

She was knee deep

Replaying her day

As he hit the doorway

Love is caution

When communication is broken

Negative energy surrounds

Discouraged to turn it around

Unable to say

He throws it away

She had good reflections
Offering her compassion

Lost in his world

Breaking her pearl

Searching inside

Her soul had died

Lost in his maze

Stuck in his ways

Two joined as one

A love like an ocean

Now a turning point

One to disappoint

Neglecting her existence

She reminisces

Bottled inside

No longer to hide

Letting go of her wounds

He would howl soon

Against a wall

Starting to fall

A glimpse of hope

Then cut by a rope

If she walks up to leave

Give her space to grieve

If you try to control her

She will go further

If you try to hold her

She will love you better

None of this is happening

The memories she's recapturing

Actions perceived

Blindness will bleed

A beautiful soul

A heart of gold

Holding on to a window

A mural of sorrow

A fairy-tale dream

A dried-up stream

What's meant to be will be

No one can see

To a world unknown

A mind was drowned...

Learning to fly

Here on this earth as human beings

Were leaning each day how to grow our wings

The first thing we see at birth is a light

A brand-new world having to fight

As we strive to figure out this life

Our past can cut us like a knife

New beginnings can halt us in place

Broken hearts can bring tears to our face

Each day as we breath and hammer our way

The sunshine can turn dark and gray

The negative mind can play a game

Breaking us down just the same

Believing the illusions, we lose our faith

Our mental ability is now at stake

Exhausted and weak we neglect our care

In anger we scream this just isn't fair

No comfort is found in our world outside

Lost in despair with our eagle eye

An earthquake shakes us to the ground

Against ourselves it's a battle ground

A helping hand could help us cope

The dullness of the dark losing hope

At odds with the demons of the night

Shattered souls look for an inner light

A gentle heart could mend the scars

A beautiful soul leading us to the stars

When the load is over your shoulder

When your world has gotten colder

Reach for me I'll be there

Reach for me I'll show you I care

Never give up on who you are

No matter how deep the scar

All of us here on earth are learning to fly
Don't let the beauty pass you by...

Turn the tide
In the valley over the hill

Rested a heart that overfilled

Inside of her castle

The emotions rattled

She lit a candle

Her hands were fragile

With a paper and pen

Writing her pain, in hopes to mend

Her tears were dry

Her eyes could not cry

Stitching her wounds gently

Over seeing her beauty

Alone in the darkness

Musing of a sweet caress

Someone to hold her

A soft touch to surround her

Deep in her thoughts

An image was loss

Desires took over

Her need was stronger

Painting in her mind

A vision so fine

Carefully approaching her

He pulled her closer

Placing his hands on her hair

Kissing her lips with flair Arousing every inch of her body

He made her feel pretty

Breathing softly on her skin

Her battle with him she could win

Then out of nowhere

She felt cold air

Her mind was burned out

Her life in doubt

Demoralized even more

A heart was at war

Rearranging the pieces to fit
on the face of it

Escaping her mind and body

An affliction hurt badly

Enjoying her company

Still, she felt lonely

Healing into another

As this was better

The person she was, no longer remained

A new girl was found the same

The moment had passed

She was whole at last

Turn the tide

Look inside

Find your pride ....

A million tears

Is it too late to turn this life around?

Can my love move the earth without sound?

Will the heaven hear my call?

Will billions more fall?

The truth lies hidden in the dark world

Flashing lights unlike before

Shamed away in my beliefs

Awaken in my grief

Human tears flood the ground

Lies evaporate all around

A ticking time bomb is set

The angle holds regret

To break the trance what will it take

How many more will make a mistake

Courage holds me in my place

To fear no one, I must face

The pieces are scattered on the floor

Make a move and hit the core

Hold your peace until the end

Hurting hearts have lost a friend

Empowered souls United

Together a world they've lighted

In hope and strength uplifted

Against the others blacklisted

Darkness will find the light

The goodness will reunite

Hold tight your faith

Beautiful souls will escape....

Inside the Chamber's of Your Heart

Carried down the river, I can't see

What has come over me

Seen the shadow of a Hollow

Down the stream I heard an echo

Save me from the danger

This time I'm going under

The falls are coming soon

The flashbacks have me doomed

Hear the cries I let out
Hear what this life was about

The adrenaline holds me fast

Sunken inside of the past

Break out from the demon's hand

Release yourself from the desert sand

Rise above the water

Pull yourself together

The time has come to pass

The stream is coming fast

Brace against the tide

Release the tears inside

Let the river bring you high

Let your tear fall and cry

You armor will surround

A meaning more profound

Humble and fierce

The warrior will pierce

In the chambers of your heart

A storm will come apart

In your castle you'll see

Your soul will be set free....

Breaking through the glass

Bleeding inside your soul

A world outside has turned so cold

A heavy feeling on your heart

In silence you're tearing apart

The teardrops fall warmly on your face

Pure and divine the emotions take place

A whisper is heard to take it slow

When your pain starts to let it go

Alone you listen to the voice

Healing inside you have no choice

When darkness grabs and holds you there

These moments can become too much to bare

It is then that we take a stand

It is then that we reach for a hand

If the hand is nowhere to be around

If you feel like no hope can be found

Be your Savior in the dark

Be the candle and flame that spark

Let your heart be set free

Let your eyes finally see

Creeping in through your room

A healing power you'll feel soon

Pat yourself on the back

Cut yourself some slack

In life we have lessons

In life we find the reasons

Stand up and wipe your tears

Break through all your fears

Open the door and walk outside

Crank the music and go for a ride

Feel the breeze caressing your cheeks

Notice this moment you seek

Your love for humanity is real

Follow your heart and feel

The energy around you is moving

The inside of you is changing

Breaking through the glass you embrace
Your freedom, you finally taste

Unchained

Darkness follows in your steps

Emotions are just a wreck

Determined to be steady on your feet

Faith is what you seek

Torn inside your soul

A story never told

The mind can trample

Leaving your world unravel

Fighting against the clock

Hoping an opportunity would knock

Doors close and leave you there

A feeling you cannot bare

On the edge of a small thread

Remembering what was said

Evil lingers all around

Leaving you in tears to drown

In a state of mind control

What happens next was not foretold

Courage confronts you in the dark

You felt it in your heart

Silencing the voice astoned

A victory had overthrown

Struggles will be no more

Your stronger than before

Your eyes have found a light

This chapter you'll rewrite

When you find yourself alone

Fear not the unknown

One life you have to live

Give it all you have to give

Break the chains that bind

Take the leap and climb

Surround yourself with love

The soul of hope and dove

Your life has come unchained

As powerful as a lion's mane....

A Soul's Journey

Struggling in a web

Unable to comprehend

Time is a capsule of sand

Passing through your hand

Castles swept away

I wish that they could stay

Searching for the reason

Dug deep through every season

The moment came and passed

Turning directions at last

Awakening to the world outside

Healing came inside

Seeing through my heart

The pieces fell apart

Planting the seeds of survival

Healing through a new revival

A new me had carried on

The soul was too far gone

The pain had buried me

This I could not see
When I felt it in my heart
My whole world had restart

Free to roam again

An old me had to end

Blessed in ways unknown

My gift to the world I shown

A soul's journey begun

With me smiling through the sun....

Shadow of a doubt

Walking through a dark tunnel

Like a horse without a saddle

An emptiness inside my soul

Living in a world so cold

Trembling at every corner

Hoping this life will get better

The thoughts ignite in flames

As for me I'm not the same

Lost inside my thoughts

Feeling so distraught

Crying tears of pain

Drowning myself in rain

Holding on to a tunnel wall

Afraid I might just fall

Unable to see and feel

Nothing for me is real

The wind blows through the air

My will to live - I know it's there

Give me strength to carry on

Give me a sign the world's not gone

On these knees crawling out

The Shadow had me in doubt

Adjusting myself to gravity

The light I finally see

The devil was laughing at me

In the darkness I could not see

An angel came to light my way

My mind was set in time I stay

Tunnels are dark

When a new journey starts

After a while you get to see

The beauty that lies in me

Straighten your crown

Now your light has been found....

Hold on to your beautiful crown

In a cold world made of stone

Alone inside your home

Holding on to what is left

In a shattered heart trying your best

If only humans had wings to fly

I wouldn't be here in my room to cry

I'd fly through the midnight sky

Flying above the clouds so high

Broken to pieces falling apart

A pain that stabs, through my heart

Crawling on my knees

In a body that starts to freeze

Calling out for an angel tonight

Calling out that something ain't right

A world outside I ain't recognize

A world in shambles covered in lies

Screaming now without a sound

The mind is fooling me around

A restless body cannot sleep

This darkness has sunk me so deep

Torn apart inside

Wanting someone here by my side

When our world is spinning around

When all hope seems gone

Focus, Reset and breath

Fight all evil that feed

Be brave, be bold and strong

Hold on to your beautiful crown

When life brings you down

It is in those darkest moments that we are found....

Wake the lions

The clock is ticking for humanity

The race is getting ugly

Lies continue to circulate

Their demands begin to escalate

Unseen, unheard never in a lifetime

The Warriors against a wartime

Inside our minds it over stimulates

Finding ways around these mandates

Covered up by misconceptions

Around every corner there are sanctions

The separation builds a wall

Human beings begin to fall

Heartbroken and mourning

The nightmare's never ending

A human touch is greatly needed

Alone and defeated

Crimes against humanity

Taking away our sanity

Tearing at our hearts

Our world is falling apart

No choice given for the jab

Fighting darkness giving it all we have

Immunity was born in us

Our gov we don't trust

Censored to share the truth

Our words set on mute

Hitting a brick wall

Inside our skin we start to crawl

Hands together praying hard

The pain is real it bombards

Alone and scared

Feeling so despaired

Big pharma's up our ass

This jab, no thanks I'll pass

The science makes no sense

The billionaire's on defense

The time has come and gone

Our society has withdrawn

Crossing through our road

Warriors of gold

Like minded all the way

Our pack is here to stay

Fighting tyranny through and through

The madness we must undue

Standing up for what is right

Waking other's is a fight

Hidden by the truth to see

In battles we disagree

Hope is lost, hope is found

Our will to live is profound

If we stand the game is over

Together we are stronger

So, take my hand and bleed with me

The lions are here to set us free

The moon is gleaming

The light is shining

Lift your armor

Let's fight together...

Holding it together

A world crumbles and falls from the sky

As she inhales and exhales, it multiplies

The impact is felt from ocean to ocean

The devastation each day it deepens

Traveling intensely like a freight train Driving her emotions insane

In solitary she retreats to think

Refusing to give up to a weakest link

Gathering her thoughts, pausing to see

How her life, got to be so heavy

Blessed by her writing and poetry

As it balances her peace and harmony

As the stars shine less and less

As her essence is deterrent by a test

An angel whispers in her ear

As the devil disappears

One fills her with hope

The other strangles her throat

Torn between right and wrong

Padding back and forth like a ping pong Kneeling to her knees in mental collapse

Pulling herself up by her bootstraps

She has learned how to survive

In a world that eats you alive

She will hold it together

Never to give up or surrender...

Frame of mind

Closing her eyes as she takes a sigh

A way of life came to say goodbye

Her vital force was forever changed

In the uncertainty, she'd rearrange

When rain clouds are dark blue

In shadows of doubt, she will see it through No one can predict the future

No one can envision the architecture

She dives into the core of her soul

Carving down to her deep hole

Ancient wounds broken into fragments

She would Harrow and cultivate segments

Knowing that a seed could traumatize

In her healing she would plant wise

A past is unchanging

This can be discouraging

Recollect and try to undo

Impossible, unless you bring light into

She grabbed her shield and teared it down

Hidden from view, she'd reveal it now

There are no parades or drums around

As she braces on her merry go round

Tears fall from her hazel eyes

Releasing pain as there crystallized

Unchaperoned, she glows in the moonless

Confident that a kindred soul will have humbleness

In her new frame of mind

Aspiring for a love to intertwine...

Victorious

A body was designed to handle pain

In a pharmaceutical world insane

A list of side effects is long

An outcome inside that could go wrong

So, she suck's up the suffering

Throbbing, aching and excruciating

A talk show host lives her torture

Placing a weapon on his head in a corner

Thank God he didn't pull the trigger

As the Angel came to whisper

Like her pushing forward

To give up would be coward

The invisible is not seen by others

In agony, they stand as soldiers

Prepared to defeat its ugliness

Courageously fighting for healthiness

A pill she will never swallow

Even if the night gets hollow

Injections were limited

As she refused to be experimented

Alternative medicine and medicinal hop

She would give it all one shot

Spaced out in her trial of weed

Writing Porn in lieu of Poem on her feed

She laughed it out loud

As her head was in the cloud

Everyday battling the dark

Waiting for a homerun in the ballpark

A loved one on three patches of Morphine

Not her she would intervene

When your road gives you no choice

Stand up and be your own voice

Through the suffering that is tortuous

You have the power to be Victorious...

Endearment

Climbing Mount Everest on firm footing

Through her shadow, she's wondering

Her voice echoed on the high hills

As she was learning new survival skills

The air was invigorating

A new life was beginning

Single handed her path became

Through her sadness, she overcame

Setting up tent at the very top

To find her destiny, she will never stop

In solitary, she built a campfire

Feeling a warmth through the fire

After descending the steep mountain

She anticipates, finding a companion

As daybreak arrived

She had packed her stuff and drived

In her heartbreak she had been fearful

In her newfound dream she is graceful

Footloose and fancy free

She imagined a love that is heavenly

A man who shows appreciation

A man who is impassioned

Laying her down in a bed of roses

With a kiss and a touch of sweetness

Feeling deep down to his soul

A relish that is whole

Connecting with a heart that's pure

Under the sun she'd endure

One glance in his eyes

A touch of his lips beautifies

A love sensational and seductive

Finding the right one, she'd be selective

Laying her head against his chest

On the beating of his heart, she'd rest

Amorous and arousing

In her imagination astounding

If only she knew where to find him

An essence like her of individualism

Two lovers whispering endearment

Unfettered together in wonderment...

Permanent wave

She may not know where she is going

Or when her heart could stop beating

She may not know what tomorrow will bring

Or if it will be tearful or breathtaking

She wakes up daily giving it her all

Even if she trips and falls

She cries tears of joy and pain

None of which is ever the same

As she watched the world collapse

In her dark moments of relapse

She fought with all her might

Carrying hope and a candlelight

She was put down and yelled at

Unable to please everyone, she clapped

Turning the page on those who drowned her

Opening the door to those in deep water

In a world lacking compassion

She will give her devotion

In blood, sweat and tears

In her darkest of fears

She will keep on fighting

She will break the walls binding

Que sera sera,

Whatever will be will be

She may not have all the answers

She may not be able to stop all disasters

All she can do is be brave

And send out love in a permanent wave...

Motherload

City lights illuminate the night

As she travels through the green light

Her road is narrow and uncertain

As her old dreams had cancellations

Through these times we live in

A love became overbearing

Seeing no light at the end of her tunnel

In solus building now her castle

Sometimes that's the way things go

Even Though it fills her with sorrow

When she saw the glass half empty

When her heart became too heavy

She broke a chain that was comfortable

As her matrimony was unfathomable

As she digged in her heels

She took on her own steering wheel

Looking through colored glasses

She had overlooked weaknesses

In her utmost discouragement

Her courage was transparent

That's the way the cookie crumbles

She will deal a new hand and shuffle

If one loves her dearly

He would admit his faults honestly

If one had her best interest at heart

He would make her center, in his fine art

If one could understand her silence

He would show her patience

She made a hard decision

To leave her lifelong companion

She cried her eyes out

As she had loved him no doubt

The flame had burned down

Now the circus was leaving town

A love once, so desired

Had left her uninspired

She took the leap forward

In her heartbreak, soft hearted

Down the yellow brick road

She would find her motherload ...

Spiritually inclined

A Universe turns inside her mind

Saving humanity, she was left behind

A genuine heart that bled so deep

Turning her cheek, they were sound asleep

A floor cracks as she paces back

She's wide awake and off track

She tries hard to connect the dots

As there is uncertainty in her blind spots

She takes a deep breath of fresh air

As her core starts to tear

A woman of strength and virtue

In a world that turned her black and blue

She knows what she needs to do

It's an emotional wheel to go through

An arrow shot through her chamber

She will be different now forever

A wired fence will be built around

Until an authentic soul can be found

A guardian will protect her cage

Until she's ready to turn the page

A beautiful chapter she'll rewrite

Making this one a firing light

If one tries to saddle her eye

May this one never make her cry

As she builds herself high

For her life to be beautify

If one believes he is right for her

May he always bring her pleasure

Some will feel like a fish out of water

As she is a far cry from the other

As the universe turns inside her mind

Is there one who is Spiritually inclined...

Chasing the wind

A road had changed fast

In the blink of an eye by contrast

Tables had turned over

In heartbreak, she'd recover

Where there's a will, there's a way

Now courageous in her turn away

No tears could hold her back

As she was now on the right track

Everything in life happens for a reason

She told herself, through this separation

In her melancholy, she had hope

As she had been, at the end of her rope

Finding her wings again

She'd enjoy a fine champagne

In a storm that took her by surprise

There were no reasons, left to try

As the shadows appeared in her view

This needed her attention to look through

Dismissed for far too long

In his arms no more she belonged

A love had gone sour

On her own she'd be much better

The first step is truly the hardest

She will need to stay focus

In a cruel world outside her window

Headstrong, she will heal her sorrow

Walking away from all she knew

The life ahead there was no preview

Aspiring for beautiful things

In a world now that is puzzling

Chasing the wind

Leaving her bare skinned

Now she is bound and determined...

Impassioned

Standing on the edge of the fast-moving water

In her eleventh hour, feeling so much pleasure

The mist caressed her face

The soft water she could taste

Beauty once darkened around her

In her trauma, was a reminder

Through a new lens, she could see

Her soul would heal in her company

Stepping down from the cascade

She learns to take down her barricades

A divine heart that loved the world

Had abandoned, this lovely girl

Some could not see through her red tape

Or the nightmare confronted, to escape

Driving to her cabin in the woods

Dreaming as one always should

By the sand, she placed her feet

Warm and invigorating, she took a seat

Peace flowed through her mind

One day with the universe, she'd align

Experience's gathering, in Synchronicities

Signs flowing with intensities

A mystery of life perplexed her

A delicate flower, inside her chamber

As the water covered her body in sand

In the distance, she saw a man

An illusion perhaps in her mind

A wish perhaps in her lifetime

Her eyes kept a steady gaze

As the vision came her way

He was handsome and sweet, as he arrived

She pinched herself to see if she was alive

Bending down to sit by the water

Her heart started to flutter

Gazing in her eyes

He felt the night sky

Touching his lips on hers

He felt her wings of feather

Pulling him closer to her

She felt she could stay here forever

Softly touching his skin

She felt him coming in

Aroused unlike before

Had she found her amore?

Kindly he lifted her off the sand

Holding her close, he held her hand

Walking up to the cabin

Two souls were connecting

In a poet's story it was written

Two hearts were impassioned...

Emptiness

In the night sky that shines above us

Her strong spirit was turning to dust

She could move heaven and earth

If only she could see her worth

Placing her heart and soul into everything

To some this meant nothing

Soul seeking for days on end

Through her poetry, she would send

For every word, she writes in ink

Her mind will rethink

An enemy of war inside her mind

Like a puzzle of seek and find

On the outer layer of her eyes

A world hides in fake disguise

She was stitched different from the rest

Her uniqueness, was always a test

A secret diary, held her pain

The hidden darkness of torrential rain

Scars of old, pierced her heart

Visions so near teared her apart

Everyday is a battle within

Some days she's not sure if she'll win

A fire breathing dragon

Sends flames in her foundation

Tapping her shoulder to carry on

Starting fresh at the crack of dawn

She knows that life has a funny way

To reel you in when you Castaway

A hockey bag she drags around

Heavy thoughts, bring her down

If one plus one makes two

In baby steps, one could undo

It's human to cry and shed tears

It's human to lose our cheer

If a wagon loses its wheel

We fix it, it's no big deal

When our soul faces difficulties

Like a Carpenter, we must fix discrepancies

She will sail on the beautiful seas

She will one day caress it's breeze

Emptiness felt inside

With a brave heart, she will override...

Be brave enough

Signs are everywhere we go

Most of us don't even know

A blind eye is turned

Ironically a change we yearn

On a falling star, we wish

For a life of bliss

Inside ourselves we hide secrets
Wasting so many precious minutes

What if we told it like it is?

What if we didn't butter it with cheez whiz

If you love someone say it

Connect with there inner spirit

If you think he's hot or she's sexy

Maybe the two of you should gain clarity

In love with the soul or body

An internal feeling is more heavenly

For the core will not grow old

Where a face and body will fold

Time is unknown

A precious gemstone

When the universe speaks to you

Sit down and have a rendezvous

Absorb the energy within

Don't look for a fairy-tale magazine

The answers lie within you

All around it speaks to you

Walk a mile to unwind

Do it before your own time

No one knows what lies ahead

We are created of our bread

Sour if one chooses

An alarm repeatedly on snoozes

Take a chance and speak your mind

You're the coach to redesign

Be brave enough

Don't sweat the small stuff ...

Letting go

Would you remember my name?

Would your feelings be the same?

Dancing in the dark

Ripping out her heart

When she turned the other cheek

In revenge you seek

You did not see her crying

You did not see what she was needing

In her muted world, you could not tell

A love had fell inside a well

As you look in the mirror
Do you not see terror

Can you not see your part?

Pretending to be perfect, this ain't smart

Oh! Contraire, it reflects your darkness

A side dish through your sweetness

Your words were sugar

Trying to fool others as a charmer

Seen through the illusion

Time wasted on a wrong connection

What made me blind?

Now it's crystal clear in my mind

Now I'm letting go

A love out the window

No questions remain

As she is no longer the same

In her own company at peace
Enjoying her delicacies

A Great Golden Butterfly

In a cocoon desiring to grow her wings

Chanting a lovely melody, she sings

A beautiful butterfly, she would be

If only her life could be a cup of tea

Rock bottom cuffs her good

A prison molding wood

Inside a chamber of thoughts

Growing painfully, distraught

Wishing for it all to be gone

In blood and tears holding on

Making way for a soul to bloom

The wind blows on her cocoon

In this magnificent maple tree

Dripping syrup as sweet as can be

A being fights against the dark

Trapped inside this bark

A transformation so hidden

Solus in her division

It is unseen by others

Powerless without wings and feathers

Claustrophobic she becomes

As she hears the marching drums Screaming for an SOS

Anxiously waiting, in her cocktail dress

The growth of a caterpillar

Most would prefer, to gaze at the Saddle River

It is a battle no one can see

Through the caterpillar's journey

If the cocoon revealed its flaws

If the cocoon had an unlucky straw

Would the resistance transpose?

Would her soul be foreclosed?

Tis a judgmental society we breed

In our differences we feed

Dismantling all that is delicate

In our morals misinterpreted

A fissure begins inside her shell

Cracking open her bodyshell

Opening up slowly, she is dainty

Surfacing from a place of uncertainty

Beautiful and Colorful

She is spiritual

A flower in the sky

A Great Golden Butterfly...

Beautiful creations

Round and round

Like a marigold round

A rollercoaster ride

In a darkness, that won't subside

Although rainbows appear

Clouds roll in, her atmosphere

One minute it's beautiful

The next it's tribunal

Love cannot dominate

If one cannot communicate

Slipping on a banana peel

Every bruise, she feels

Limping on her tight rope

Inside her throat, she chokes

She wants to be heard

Not judged in her words

Silenced by assumptions

Overlooked by deceptions

Charlotte's Web caught her good

She was tangled, misunderstood

Cloud nine was a mirage
Disguised in her camouflage

Buttercups are sweet

She'd travel there bare feet

Squishing grapes to make wine

A real heart that's divine

Imperfect we all are

Each one of us have scars

Forgive and never forget

A past holds regret

She wants to kiss a Blueberry Tree

In tranquility and love, wanting to see

Climbing uphill and rolling down

Enjoying life without a frown

What a beautiful life it would be

If the troubles could set her free

For now, she writes on her loveseat

Musing of another's heartbeat

In her figment of imagination

Aspiring to beautiful creations...

Attaching her feather wings

The shadow of one, makes her shaded

Dimming her light, she becomes frustrated

The strength she gives to stand strong

Is blown off as one comes along

True colors splashed on her face

Hanging around in her breathing space

Taking shelter to protect her soul

As one lacked self control

A thermostat could not rise high enough Icicles formed to make it rough

Stepping back, farther to see

A love had turned melancholy

As her heart shattered inside

She wanted to run to the countryside

Peace of mind, she needed now

As her emotions were overflowed

Soon the gate would open up

A life from scratch, she'd buildup

In her newfound chateau

She will become her own superhero

The pain that was meant to destroy her

Will be the seeds she plants to remind her

For in her most tribulant of times

Not even the earth could rewind

Heaving forward in her new adventure

The wisdom learned will make her wiser

The beauty in her core

Will grow stronger

As she lays her head on her cradle

Deep inside, her heart is fragile

Setting her eyes on the ceiling

As the teardrops come pouring

A darling saw a story ending

In her darkness was a new beginning

Attaching her feather wings

In her spiritual awakening...

Deep Affection

The morning smelt of fresh grass

Where she had imagined she'd raise her glass

The sky was a beautiful blue

Not a cloud in sight, it was true

She was surrounded by a new light

A story, she would rewrite

Remembering the tears she had shed

Remembering the time her heart had bled

She knew now, she was headstrong

She had survived the storm, that came along

Picking up each diamond that fell down

In her sorrow, she had never back down

A deep breath, she finally took

As she took out, her lovely notebook

Her pen no longer wrote of woe

For in her mind passion stroke too

Loveable, she became to one

A story of love had begun

In her careful indulgence

Choosing one of confidence

One of encouragement

One of equivalence

A companion of genuine moral's

One who could withstand a few quarrels

One who understood her goodwill

One where her heart could overfill

With beauty, laughter and devoutness

Lighting one candle with matches

With her notepad, keeping her company

Bringing her a love of ecstasy

The morning smelt of fresh grass

In deep Affection, they were one at last...

Loveless

Scrolling through an app, for a miracle

An answer to heal her struggles

On social media really?

It's an obsession sadly

All the beautiful souls who are lonely

Joined on here to find friends that are lovely

A master plan is needed

To figure out where she's headed

A palace came apart

Crumbling pieces in her heart

Coming down in torrents

In an awakening moment

Alone in the darkest of nights

Hoping for the Northern Lights

Knowing how many beans make one

Taking steps to a rising sun

Signing away her past

Threading the needle at last

Bursting into tears once more

Saying goodbye to her amore

The core will bleed for some time

Her generosity will last for a lifetime

On her journey loveless

One can only hope, it will be Beauteous...

Lamb's Ears

As memories resurface

The inevitable proves disastrous

Instead of mourning and moving on

She hid it under the carpet and held on

The vision was painful

The recollection was dreadful

Blaming herself for the events

Against herself was a sentence

Carrying the load throughout her life

The devastation, cut her like a knife

Placing pity on the offender

Disregarding herself, she sunk further

Plummeting down the stairway

As she tried to give his crime away

In night terrors, laughing in an orange suit
As though he had taken away, her forbidden fruit

This memory haunted her gravely

For the years, she tried to bury

Bursting into tears in her bathroom

Concealing her face in her powder room

Although this tragedy was enough

More was forthcoming to make it rough

Tearing at her innocence was hauntable

A defenseless time was irreversible

Reliving this ordeal over and over

A weight she carried, on her shoulder

In adulthood painting life with her past

Anxiety and pain held her fast

Combined with lesions to distort it all

It managed to destroy her firewall

A truth undisclosed to her

Selfishly he kept, inside his chamber

As the paradox was exposed

The veracity in her mind, strongly opposed

Placing her foot in her grave

She retrieved to a dark storm cave

Coming to terms with the news

Unhealed in her scars, it continued

As the monsters drowned her whole

She needed to be one with her heart and soul

Unbuttoning her pain, she unleashed

The lessons of life, no more to teach

As her heart opens on Lamb's Ears

In time she will feel the demons disappear

Ambivalence

The sun breaks on the morning sky

A woman rises from a goodnights cry

Pouring herself a coffee

In her messy hair, still pretty

She brings her coffee to the veranda

Crossed in love, still holding charisma

A morning breeze brings her a chill

Strong minded in her will

A hummingbird bird sits by her window

The pain for her is hard to swallow

Admiring the beauty of this creature

Imagining now, her next adventure

Bad habits comfort her now

As the days ahead she's not sure how

Thin and fragile in her body

The wound inside is heavy

A splash of distress writing in pen

Each word planted inside her garden

She wanted badly to erase the wrong

She wanted badly to stop this sad song

Crying as though her heart would break

Anger geared towards the government. mistakes

Tearing down her walls, unfathomable

To make sense of all this is questionable

Reasons of life were right

Humanity was worth the fight

Clouds roll over to hide the sun

A vision she could not outrun

To get the ducks in a row

She would need to cleanse her sorrow

Torn between her thoughts and core

The answers were clear, turning back nevermore

A feeling of Ambivalence

For now, it will take patience...

Fighting chance

One can only wonder, if there's only one life

One can only imagine, if there is an after life

A chance encounter in person, virtually

A meaning, a purpose one wonders truly

In total darkness a mind can empty

A heart can beat rapidly

Answers of life are not written in stone

They are felt deep in our bones

In companionship you can forget

Yourself in this safety net

When true colors are exposed

Signs can slip from under your nose

Her imagination was used against her

Her creative mind was being tortured

As the dark had been a focus

She escaped to be mysterious

On an island of her own

Inside her soul she had grown

The damage would need repairs

She'd need someone that truly cares
The wrong would need a right

A flame in the dark she'd ignite

In distance it would be

As she needed to be set free

On her new voyage through the valley's

She set out in curiosity

Uncertainty now as she steers the wheel

Only time now would reveal

In love if she took a chance

In her eyes would he glance

If she ran into his arms

Would he be her lucky charm?

Will she be nervous and stutter her words?

Would they become one as love birds

If she let him see her dark

Would he leave her when she'd start?

Through this valley of the unknown

Would his soul be her own?

If she let him touch her inside

Would he run right after and hide

Would there be a Fighting chance?

Would she finally learn to dance...?

Flight of imagination

She can hear cries in the night

She can feel her chest squeezing tight

Teardrops fall like a faucet

The light of love, holds no regret

For she knows, she was needed

Even if inside she bleeded

Some say she is an angel

Her eyes glow of hazel

Some say she was the light

Now she fights, day and night

A funnel cloud arrived

In her shadow, was a surprise

As the winds were howling strong

In her heartache, she stood her ground

Underneath her breath she sighed

Trying to feel the heart that died

In her weaknesses of tomorrows

In her deepest of sorrows

She searches for the horizon

She yearns for a touch of passion

For it is in her mind

Where the answers, she will find

When it gets too much

She retrieves and imagines lush

A woman can bleed deeply

A woman can love truly

She was that woman

A poet full of passion

She was different than most

An outcast floating along the coast

She did not flinch to fit in

She was quite unique within

Even the mockingbird could not sing
The pain she had quavered in her writing

To kiss a fool, she would not

To kiss a sweetheart, she was taught

Scars had followed her soul

The hardships hidden, not told

Feeling nauseous as she wakes

The ground shakes like an earthquake

Tension builds leaving her shaking

Everything now she is questioning

Calm in her words, as she speaks

As she struggles to stay on her feet

Everyday is a victory closer

As she stitches back her feather

Broken Wings in her flight of imagination

To rebuild her life, will be her greatest creation...

Philosopher

A heart and a beautiful mind at war

A story like never before

Emotional baggage sowed to lesions

The audience, makes assumptions

Digging her grave inside the ground

As the news leaves her astound

To walk in her shoes is invisible

A vision only seen, that is personal

Deemed by many

Her shoes are muddy

She knows far too well

This unpredictability, cannot foretell

Defeated in her desperation

Unable to control the deterioration

Knee high, in her crawl space

The Devil's hand, she had to face

Unbearably writing her pain, with her fingers

On this wooden table leaving her splinters

Cascading through her heart

Booster cables, she'd need to restart

Relentless in her grief

A wizard was in disbelief

A heart and mind collided

A catastrophe hard handed

Finding the meaning of life a philosopher
She was amazing but she couldn't remember...

A House of cards

Seated here in quietness

The depletion leaves her powerless

A divide outside her doors

Has changed her life forever more

Heightening the weaken minds

Against the enemy that charged behind

Sending light, through a mobile phone

A sole intention, for those alone

Preoccupied in her mission of combat

Blindfolded just like that

As she hung her lanterns in the air

A simple act of kindness, barred her there

The clock struck a nasty chord

As he wrote her pain, on his chalkboard

The notes he took while she tried to heal

Sent her a missile, where she used to feel

Sharp edges of glass dividing

In her world transforming

At a loss, now for words

As her soul tries to move forward

Seated here in quietness

A house of cards was passionless...

Naked Eye

Never once giving up on anyone

A cold world made assumptions

Overburdened by her trauma

Increasing daily in her aroma

As soft as a baby's skin

Against all odds, she was determined

Even when she hit the floor

And her heart could take no more

The tears could not sustain

Her built in storm drain

Truth can be told of her devastations

A will to live, a tribulation

In her reflection, a mirror of lies

Her innocence compromised

As the wheel keeps on turning

This entanglement, is more perplexing

She will rise in time like the Phoenix

Arousing a fire through her match sticks

Light as a feather, she will move about

Granting herself space, to cry it out

The heavenly body will turn once more

Collecting her shells along the seashore

In clear conscience

Through life altering experience

She will be implacable

In this storm so torrential

The transformation of a Butterfly

She discerned, through the Naked Eye...

Pearl white

A road can look dark

When it begins from the start

Leaving memories behind

As there is no more here to find

Panning at your chest

You find it hard to rest

Looking for distractions

As you heal through creations

Aspiring for a sign of optimism

As a new journey can be worrisome

Knowing in your heart, the decision was right
In somber, you will find a guiding light

A world can be lonely

In your own company

Anxiously pondering, who you could trust

Maybe a beautiful soul who has a gentle touch

How would one know if this person is right?

How does one tell, who would be worth the fight?

To love someone again could be possible

Only question is who would be worth the trouble

Movies always make love scenes so magical

Reality is, make believe is unpractical

A fire on a screen of passion

Is better felt real, in satisfaction

When the darkness washes over you

May you find a love that is true

May you feel alive once again

May the sweetness be like champagne

Dance to the beat of the rhythm out loud

Forgive your past, as imperfections are aloud

A recollection is different for all

Promise yourself, you will never fall

The ability to cleanse yourself

Is a lovely gift, to give oneself

When the water is purified

One's life can become pearl white ...

Benevolence

Time is undermined

In a world where people are scrambling

She once occupied that space

Where she thought life was a race

Lessons and heartaches can illuminate

Awakening our souls to create

In low spirits, we can drown

In pizzazz we can be found

When we have graciousness

We can bring a new level of consciousness

When we are merely focused on outer beauty

We may brush off the medicine that sweetens the tea

Coffee is planted as tiny seeds

When it blooms, an aroma we breathe

If only one star could light up the sky

Imagine what a sky full of stars could gratify

Mental suffering is ignored

Until one life, is no more

If we fabricate, a planet of delight

Could we save humanity from the end of light?

Sweetness shared amongst every last one

Would light an ocean like a beacon

Passionate emotions can be exciting

Uniting this world to be more loving

Wishful thinking can move mountains

Nourishing our lips like a water fountain

As the world keeps on turning

As the world keeps on forgetting

In broken heartedness

She will not be venomous

In aerial flight

She will be a candlelight

As broken as her scars

She will still be a sweet candy bar

In her Benevolence

She will spread her love to humans...

Melodious

Words are an art

When they flow from the start

Exhausting it can be to dig deep

In Smokey air, a pen and hand will meet

Only when the mind is balanced

Will the words of a poet dance?

Only when the mind is at war

Will the tears spill from the core?

In darkness, a pen has no glow

It is the poet's soul that will show

In the cloudiest of nights

A poet will ignite

For it is through suffering

That a poet can sing

A melody so enchanting

Leaving the reader wondering

When will it rain again?

For a poet's words to bend

Will it be a sad story?

Will it bring, a tale of pity?

Imagine if the poet felt inspired

And the words could spark fire

Knowledge and imagination

Such a beautiful creation

To hear the words of an artist

Sealed not once but twice in bliss

Love, Agony and Tragedy

Melodious to a poet's true beauty...

Shake your tree

Hands tied behind her back

A choice of words, she lacked

Bewildered in dark blue

Like a princess losing her shoe

Scrubbing down, on her hands and knees

As her shattered heart, grieves

She mused, at the essence she faced

As many had tried to tie her lace

Restrained from reaching out

At a loss, feeling worn out

Not able to express

Feeling defeated and distressed

Heavy handed in her tubing

She feels her head pounding

At arm's, with so much adversity

She sinks for a moment in self pity

Picking herself, off the ground

Remembering, a soul she'd found

A hidden warrior, trying to fit in

Like driving a car without an engine

Rolling down, like a marigold

Disquieted by the scars of old

In solitary, without rest

Her journey, to whom she'd confess

The imperfections and the miss
Leaning over would he kiss

The miracles and victories

Leaning over would he freeze

The courage and the heart of gold

Leaning over would he be cold

The divine and blissful smile

Leaning over would he dine

The old soul that is compassionate

Leaning over would he be affectionate

On a different path of existence

She would meet resistance

Connecting with a Belle Ame

Leaning over would he be love-some

In a sky of a bazillion stars

Leaning over would he write a memoir

Unfolding before him, a mystery
Leaning over would he shake your tree...

Wrapped up, unvanquished

In her darkest of moments

A heart was shredded to tiny fragments

Super glue was greatly needed

To put back the pieces that separated

Breathing in a different air

Through clouded lenses, she stared

A vision of the unknown

As she departs partially, a road alone

Without peace in her thoughts

As the leaves fall from her flowerpots

A mind overthinks

Writing through invisible ink

Negative vibes casting her away

As the devil wants to overstay

A destruction in her cage

Fighting endlessly to rearrange

Healing into another

As this, was a broken version of her

Seeing beyond illusions and lies

In her eyes streaming, a soul cried

To let another touch her core

Would he hurt her, furthermore?

To put a lock and throw the key
Would she behave differently?

To let her passion be forbidden

Would she become hard-bitten

At cloverleaf with her mentality

She recharges her battery

Healing herself from the pain

Her heart of light, would remain

Wrapped up, unvanquished

An open heart one day she'd cherish

Strong will

At cross purposes

A mind is restless

Floating outside her body

Not feeling anything really

A heart that once beat internally

Was separated carelessly

Uncertain how to proceed ahead
Subconsciously over her head

Performing duties once adored

Bleeding gravely in her core

A sensitive ticker, had multiplied

In delicacy, breaking down to cry

Confining in her space

In her mouth, a bitter taste

In hunger and tears

A woman disappears

Sick as a parrot, thirsty to rise

Unrepairable scars, she's paralyzed

A woman's past had oppressed

Leaving her life force in bitterness

Strong minded determined to grapple

In sunken sand, building a castle

Labeled as someone she is not
Barking up the wrong tree, she fought

Passionate and benevolent

This was her defining moment

Strong willed on her road to recovery

A woman will heal eventually...

Unpretentious

Cultivated far down to her roots

Reappearing like an old photoshoot

Imperfect by damage irreversible

In daily life unsettled

Strangled by trepidation

Protecting others in desperation

A beautiful soul unrevealed

In tribulation concealed

A challenge so circadian

Burdened in oppression

Unjustly opposed on Palisades

A war inside her escalates

Fight or flight arouses

An outcome so disastrous

In collapse attacked maliciously

Tearing her heart intensely

Setting blame on just one

Tearfully she comes undone

In her absence of light

Losing her appetite

Dipped beneath the horizon

At odds with his mind and insecurities

Blindfolded and muted

Her world is distorted

In Umbra she is desolated

There minds he manipulated

In absence of Pom Poms cheerless

In recovery she will be unpretentious...

Despondency

A pen waits for the mind to write

An umbrella of emotions holding on tight

Underground dug so deep

Hollow she seeks

Inadequately a heart stopped beating

In a glacier the temperatures freezing

Speechless in her day

Anything she had was taken away

A soldier standing still in a pose

The pain stacking tears had arose

Profound in anguish

Withdrawn she vanished

The core was displaced

Gone for now she couldn't face

Wearing her heart on her sleeve

It was smashed to smithereens

Her strong will unavailable

As her world was unpalatable

To give in and throw the towel

Impossible she was a grey owl

Adversity could knock her down

This woman, wouldn't play the clown

Descending in Despondency

Fighting against hypocrisy...

See it through...

A jet stream of words inside my head
All wanting to come out and be read

Only one hand to write was there

As I'm right-handed to be fair

In silence I was warned to stay

This was not sitting right in any way

The heavenly body concealed in fear

This I tried to steer clear

When my mouth was told to close

I was uneasy, this I had chose

As the hours and days passed to be

Self consciously I wanted to see

Deep in my thoughts I came to find

A difference in me that wasn't blind

In existence I marched a different beat

In dimension, knowledgeable I seeked
Colors were made in special shades
A language of words to kindle each page

The value of each

To the world it would teach

If we close our lips and remain silent
Will there be a loss so permanent?

Vulnerable to all that sees

Oblivious in the era of species

To all who question the beast

To all who stand against the feast

In darkness I hope my light reaches you

In darkness I hope you see it through

Until I can speak and write no more

I hope my love comforts your core...

Downfall

A roar of thunder rolled in

Separating her heart like the wall of Berlin

Electrifying was the lightning

Brought down in her awakening

Flabbergasted by the thunderclap

A vital force, now a sad sack

The inner part of her chest

Had nowhere to rest

An ocean weeping

A mind's core flooding

In her chamber of thoughts

Secluding herself, she fought

Not with words but with silence

Protecting in truth her essence

In darkness and light, she fell

Heartbroken she knew full well

Howling winds effectuated downfall
Unforeseen now in her Crystal ball...

Light a torch

When someone writes of there sorrow

Send them hope for tomorrow

When someone paints a picture of tears

Send them strength, to calm their fears

When someone sings the Blues

Offer them a band aid for there bruise

When someone speaks of desperation

Send them love and affection

When someone falls in the night

Offer them a guiding light

When someone cries tears you don't understand

Lend them compassion and your hand

When their walls come tumbling down

Send them inspiration to be found

Lend an ear to the disheartened

Listen without conversion

When someone's world mysterious

Light a torch and make it luminous...

Catharsis

Humans have grown with ideas and patterns

Around us are outer planets like Jupiter and Saturn

Most of us carry trauma and scars around

In poor advancement, leaving our faces down

The past can bring us a heavy load

The present can have us, unable to hold

Healing is not pretty, nor a walk in the park

If we keep dragging our baggage our world will be dark

Change is not an easy word to fulfill

Remaining unchanged can leave us ill

Old memories of trauma can halter growth

Leaving others around us to choke

A waterfall was made to flow

Your past was meant to let go

A boat on deck was made to anchor

Your present was made to conquer

All of us here on this earth

At one point or another have been hurt

Technology can alter reality

Compounding emotions and anxiety

Each of us can fall into affliction

Some will suffer depressions

Some will turn to addictions

The most powerful of us will seek reflection

As Stygian as this time can be

Fundamental truths can satisfy one's philosophy

Embrace the hardships as a lesson

Leading your soul into transformation

Through a healing process of Catharsis

The pearl in your garden will flourish...

A Golden key

In a world of anger and hatred

By a government dictated

Lies dispersed upon their souls

A nation left so cold

In silence writing words

Cutting you like a sword

Incapable to shed a tear

A love, bled you dear

Whispering softly to the wind

Breaking inside your skin

Reuniting human lives

To save them from their cries

An empath heart squeezed you deep

Hope was all you seeked

Torn between right and wrong

Misread by one it brought you down

Broken Wings you carried on

Forsaken, you withdrawn

A disaster in your mind

A challenge to rewind

The concrete began to crack

The walls were pulling back

Engulfed in each heartbreak

Your love couldn't take

Blind and neglected of,

Finding your mourning Dove

Your spirit illuminated the room

An aroma of sweet perfume

Glowing, from the outside

Healing gently inside

Disconnecting yourself from gloom

Flourishing like a Rosenbloom

A soul and mind set free

The awakening of a Golden key....

If you love 🖤 him forever
For seeing the future is impossible

Your flare for life is unstoppable

Through the desert sand without water

A determination gets you further

On a quest to nourish your thirst

Legs want to give out and burst

Readjusting your mindset

On your skin's eccrine sweat

Your tongue is dry as a bristle

To regain your strength is beneficial

Over the horizon is a river

The desert ends, you walk over

Refreshing you can taste

Pouring it, all over your face

Your body and mind feel different

Your light is magnetic

Moving forward on this journey

Your soul is healing beautifully

Captured by the moment

Dreaming of excitement

Fancying lush orchestrations

Inside a river basin

Setting your heart in a soul

One to make you lose control

A gentleman to hold you

A real love to pursue

If you give your heart

Will he tear it apart?

If you open your mind

Will he be kind

Will he love you, the way you are?

If you show him your scar

Will he build an empire?

If you love him forever

The future is blind

Inside of your mind

You are unstoppable

When a love is bondable...

Envisage

Overthinking in her daily existence

In this world, does she make a difference

Shooting stars to ignite the dark

Like cupid with his arrow and dart

She can't possibly save the world

No matter how high she builds a scaffold
Burdened by an unbalanced in her mind

Sometimes her milieu is hard to find

Tough as a cookie, forging ahead

Dreaming up, in her sound head

In generosity, giving to all who need

Never turning her back on all who bleed

As her life force turned a page

As she escaped from her cage

In her inner thoughts, she set free

The shackles that weighed down heavy

Taking in a new breath of life

Wanting more than a title of housewife

Examining her innermost self

Rebuilding chapters in her bookshelf

A simplicity of meat and potatoes

Heartfelt, in her consciousness Wrapping a housecoat, over her night clothes

In her bucolic surroundings, in open toes

Gazing at the star cluster

In her appetite of desire

Thinking hard about

What her life had been without

A sweet man to hold her dear

A tender soul to chase her fears

Sculpting an image of one in mind

Melting her heart as one was divine

Amorous and desirable

An inner beauty so remarkable

Touching her lips

In a sensual kiss

Feeling his essence inside her core

Undressing and teasing her even more

In her fantasy, he had graciousness

In her heartfelt desires he had kindness

To allow such though to be real

A soul in hers, she'd need to feel

Beautiful in a cloud

To break her heart, she'd disallow

Only a genuine and sincere man

Would hold her hand

Alone she will wait

For a passion of fate

Until then she'll envisage a partner
One to love her forever

The Angel revived

Obstructions scatter at every corner

Searching for answers to restore her

Looking up at the midnight sky of blue

The hardships she must undo

They say time supposed to heal

Sometimes this life is surreal

Emotions erupt in disarray

An evolution is underway

Unable to point it out

Feeling restless and in doubt

Tossing and turning in her sleep

Sinking in so deep

Living through cut ties

Giving it her all, she cries

Some days feeling down

Trying to turn it all around

Crying tears in silence

Anxious and tense

The ground starts to shake

On the edge she could break

As an empath she feels it all

In her heart a knotted ball

Haunted by her shadow

She weeps quietly in sorrow

Always lifting their broken Wings

Her life begins to sting

Capturing the energy around her

Hoping the light will reach her

Darkness feeds her soul

Alone she feels cold

Losing her balance inside the storm

Asking for the reason she was born

The book of life was never written

Old mistakes never forgotten

A heart of gold she carried heavily

Loving the world so heavenly

A beautiful mind left in vain

A beautiful mind to hide her pain

A stroke of a pen to make an art

Lighting the way through the dark

If her wounds could heal

Deep inside she could feel

The image in her mirror
Sinks her deeper

The silence in her voice

Numbs her choice

In distance separating herself

Ghosting away to dismantle her shelf

Wanting so badly to solve it now

Wanting so desperately to fix it somehow

When her walls come caving in

When her pain begins

She lets it all out to play

She surrounds herself in clay

Her sculpture is her heart

Shining brightly through the dark

A beautiful soul embarks

Rejuvenated she will start

Bringing light and love

Her soul to the earth above

An angel revived

Thanking god, she's alive …

Tribulation

A bond between two

A love once was true

She sits on her chair

Knowing well, a love had teared

Eyes fill with tears

Remembering all the years

Blowing out her candle

It was more than she could handle

His soul became altered

Self absorbed, she was bewildered

Her soul was beautiful

His actions, disregardful

Only asking for his hand

To love a gentleman

Only asking to be breathtaking

In his eyes to be amazing

Only wanting the simple things

To be a part of his wings

Only wanting to love his heart

To be a piece of his fine art

When he broke his word

He cut her up like a sword

When he tried to make a stance

There love didn't stand a chance

When he left her on her own

Inside herself she had grown

Only now it's too late

She embraced her own fate

She learnt to dance alone

She learnt to love her own

A core will heal

The tribulation she feels...

Dancing in the rain

A chest full of scars

Aspired to reach the stars

Overpowered by gray matter

Restraining to protect her

On a ghost train

Smiling through her pain

Surviving adversity

Fighting integrity

A dispirited soul

Took a stroll

Down the dark alley

She was lonely

Anxiously waiting

For something amazing

Heavy footsteps perceived

They were well conceived

No one was there

A feeling, she could not bare

Dead on her feet

Chasing a retreat

As the sun rose above

She felt unloved

Separated from Affliction

She felt a deep connection

Passion inside her soul

Trying to regain control

Feeling through literature

His words were spectacular

Although this, would never be

Her mind tried to see

Dancing in the rain

Never to be the same...

Animateness prevail

Distance apart

Protecting her heart

A candle weared down

Tearing her crown

Sleepless nights shaking

So much was happening

Vanquishing her kernel

Feeling emotional

A mind was at war

Unlike before

Wiping her tears

On deaf ears

Half asleep

She felt weak

Unhealthy to be

This she can see

Wrapped in her shawl

She leaps up tall

Energy lifts her

Right from under

Awaken inside

She is magnified

Rising upwards

She marches forward

The destiny as one

Herself she had won

Alone in her steps

Nothing to intercept

One day she will find

A love that's divine

For now, she will sail

Animateness prevails...

World shaking

Every human on earth has a purpose

Some use it to be monstrous

Some use it to make a difference

Some create havoc and subdivisions

In turmoil, a world can fall apart
Some can have a short brain fart

Other's can be manipulated

Leaving society to be segregated

A cage of thought can be conditioned

Inconceivable to be reconditioned

Those who are intractable

Are labeled as unacceptable

In the stormiest of obscurity

Beautiful souls become a minority

Bleeding in the dimness

Many can feel powerless

The cosmos send signs

Connecting souls to realign

In love, peace and harmony

Each searching for some clarity
Empathizing with one another

As we witness a disaster

Virtual hope spreads the feed

As each other's friendship we need

Lifting our spirits, as we are shun down

Strength in each other we found

Nothing happens by chance

A triumph as we're shadow banned

Stubborn as mules

By many ridiculed

Undivided we could make world-shaking changes

One day to cling United our beverages ...

Fallen

An Angel fell from the sky Today

An Angel was broken in every way

Standing Tall she had no Choice

Trying to Echo out her Voice

Perfect She tried to Be

Sadly this, she could not See

Falling from the Clouds

Would Broken Wings be Allowed?

A Caring Soul she carried Around

A Pain so deep, no reason Found

A Glimpse of Her, made her Shy

With Broken Wings, she started to Cry

Over the River She tried to Fly

Hitting rock Bottom, not knowing why

A Light appeared and guided her way

A loved one came, to save the day
With open arms, lifting her

Her life he would change forever

An Angel on Earth grew her Wing

Hope is what He would Bring...

A Dark Cloud
Holding on by a thread

A Sadness to comprehend

A downpour of tears

Overshadowing fears

Dark and shaded

Herself she hated

Out of nowhere it came

Alone and in shame

Seen many before me fall

Not me, I always stood tall

How could it be?

Strength was gone from me

Beauty faded away

Pleasure went ashtray

Cold and shaken

I was Broken

Choked up inside

Tears I tried to hide

Sorrow was real

Joy I couldn't feel

Now, I was weak

Down on my feet

What a word

So absurd

Depressed

Nothing less

A dark hole

I am told

Caught in the moment

Always a torment

A door is near

A world so dear

Breakdown

Change the frown

Hold on

Be strong

Hope, you hold

Go on, be bold

Be brave, above all

Stand Beautiful, Stand tall...

Recollection

The mind can be a disturbing place

Playing tricks on your face

The picture of Perfection is distorted

Real life images somehow forgotten

The mind can abuse you mentally

Dragging you down melancholy

The desperation of beauty you want

Blurs your vision in daunt

The mind can bring old memories

Sinking you in worries

Condemned by a portrait

Darkness in your soul, is set

The Mind can be a stage of destruction

Masking your photograph in expostulation

Restraining yourself profoundly in anguish

Now you see, a mind can be selfish

The Mind can control, it's true

Unless you see the person, you knew…

The Giant

Heaviness holds on me

A lifelong illness to carry

Sinking deep in this quicksand

Crying for help, for your hand

Thick mud feet, footprints out

Locked inside, can you hear me shout

No answers, no one found

It's dark with nothing around

Silence here, I fear

A world, so unclear

Breaking apart

Alone in my heart

Colors fade to gray

Bracing hard, I start to pray

The monster sleeps

Slowly I creep

Tears are running dry

To save myself, I must try The

giant will stand tall Never to

fall....

Burnt out Candle

Born with eyes to see the world

Beauty of life to unfold

Innocent and sweet taking steps ahead

Obeying the rules, what they said

A heart and soul

A challenge to hold

Dreams and Ambitions

Your life, the reason

Without warning you're diagnosed

Body and nerves, you choke

You fall at first, news is hard

Years pass the illness bombards

To gain victory

In a place unsteady

Answers never came

Always same

Scrambling ahead

You heard what he said

A damage mind had never gone

Multiple lesions carried on

Hope was fading

With eyes open, you were waiting

The truth in your heart

Tears you apart

A family stands to fight

By your side, searching for a light….

Hold on

How can you be strong?

When life goes all wrong

How can you stand tall?

When you try, you fall

How can you breathe? When a

mind feed

How can a wall break?

When it's too much, to take

How can wings fly?

When hope drives by

How can you go on?

When everything has gone

How can you bear this pain?

When you're drowning in rain

How can this be?

How about me

Darkness is shaded

When our light has faded

If we can reach far enough

If we can surpass what is rough

We can find strength in a human's touch...

Souls will Ponder...

Ninety-one thousand days had passed

An adoration shattered through glass

Time had been on their side

An era, on a joy ride

In ones shadow she had stood

An empath heart, she made good

On a dark cloudy night

A sweethearts soul came to light

At peace in her company

She was lovely

Self love cast about

Herself she figured out

Like an open chest overfilled

She sat by the window seal

An anchor set in motion

Casting light on her devotion

In armor and shackled gear

The open door, she had feared

Inside her cage of thought

This battle, she had fought

In a field of desire

A trail of tears brought her higher

Love shuffled in solitary

Needing only a life of simplicity

To adore again shed wait

For a man of good faith

True spirits would attach

There light would match

Souls will ponder

Until they find each other...

Southern breeze

A southern breeze arrives

Touching her inside

Butterflies around

A spirit she had found

Love would be a treat

The taste of lips so sweet

Escaping in her mind

A perception so fine

Nuzzle kiss on her neck

A firework effect

Slowly reaching in

Underneath her skin

Losing all control

Impassioned, unfold

Her heart wanted more

Of the mysterious adore

A perfect getaway
Inside her mind she'd stay

For the world outside
Made her want to hide

Darkness pulled her in A
battle she could win

A southern breeze arrives
Filling her desires ...

What is the Meaning of Life?

Is it making as much money as you can?

Is it having all the fancy name brands?

Is it falling in love and sharing dreams?

Is it challenging life till one of you screams?

Is it having kids to fill your heart?

Is it fighting for your family, to never fall apart?

Is it making mistakes to learn again and again?

Is it being perfect till the very end?

Is it laughing and sharing your all?

Is it pretending to prevent your own fall?

Is it a puzzle too great to solve?

Is it a mystery of life to resolve?

Too many questions left to answer?

Searching a lifetime for a life that's better?

Is it so easy that we can't see?

The person who knows the truth is you and me?

One life, One chance in a lifetime

Will you see the meaning of your life in time?

13 million Reasons to Live

(Published by *Polar Expression* in a book Titled *"Lean In"*)

It is now part of the national collection at Library and Archives in Ottawa for preservation in Canada's documentary history.

There are many roads

One can take to live

Sometimes life changes become an overload

Especially growing up as a Teenage Kid

Your feeling hollow, engulfed in dark faded places

Your scared to reach out

You want to shout

Tears are falling

You're breaking apart

Your forgetting

Your world becomes dark

Hold on there's a reason

13 million reasons to hold on tight

Heal from your poison your life's worth the fight

You are young and pressured

By all

Your feelings go unheard

You must stand tall

One good reason is you

The pain you feel won't last forever

You have dreams and goals waiting for you

Look up things will get better

You will graduate and leave the past behind

You'll embrace life in a way you never have before

A true love you will find

One more reason to live for

Wipe your tears and open your eyes

In the darkness there's a light you will see

Beyond social media, bullies and lies

This world is beautiful can't you see?

Reach out and get the help you need

Don't be afraid to let it out

This step you take will plant a new seed

Your life is worth it without a doubt 13

Million Reasons to Live No reasons left

to die

Together we will give

No more reasons why?

The Rose

(Published in *Whispers in the Wind*)

In the *United States*

In the world there's

Many faces,

In the world there's Many

places.

Along the path there is a rose Of

all the flowers this one I chose.

If I could light my heart would

Share,

With you a torch and make it Flare.

My thoughts in piece to make a

Picture,

My hands to hold a frame I'll Treasure.

Believing the dream of the man in

The moon,

Hoping reality will let it bloom.

The question remains, Can I have this rose?

Written by: Carole and Doris Duquette

My Hero

(Published by *Polar Expressions Publishing* in a book Titled *Broadcast*)

It is now part of the national collection at Library and Archives in Ottawa for preservation in Canada's documentary history.

A million words is not enough to describe her

Unique and kind, in my heart forever

All her life she took care of others

All her life fighting to be stronger

No matter how much pain life brought

My mother Aline was amazing, she always fought

Her smile shined from a thousand miles

Her jolly laughter, she would never hide

Night after Night caring for the vulnerable

My mother to me was so incredible

Mother your day is finally here

I know you don't drink but raise your beer

Retired at last

You can finally relax

You never knew, I never did say

Mom, you're my hero in every way...

Andy's Mountain

(Published by Polar Expressions Publishing in a

book Titled Patterns)

It is now part of the national collection at Library and Archives in Ottawa for preservation in Canada's documentary history.

Overlooking the mountains,

Sitting on the tree,

You asked me, what your dream could be?

My cries began by the thousands...

Your heart became weak

Lighting your candle, hope I would seek

A miracle now I would need...

The news arrived so quick,

We packed our bags and left real fast Was it

true, my father was so sick?

This moment to hold you, I would not pass

Over 2000 miles crossing mountains, prairies

Storm after storm defying the odds

To arrive to you, there were no boundaries

No sleep, nor food my father was the cause

In the hospital your family, your daughters stood by

You asked how far I was, when I'd arrive

My heart broke, I could not bare for you to die

This journey to you was such a long ride

I jumped from my vehicle and ran inside

There you were on the bed, these tears I could not hide

You ran your fingers through my hair

I held you close, it was so sad For you

to go, my heart would tear

On hands and knees, I begged for Dad.

Tears fell from all our eyes,

As we said our goodbyes to you

Broken inside, endless cries

Never will we forget you

Overlooking the mountains

Sitting on the tree

You asked me, what your dream could be?

My sweet father it was always you

Waiting for me on your bed

I was coming from the mountains to find you

In loving memory of Andy Duquette

November 14, 2018

Lost but never Forgotten

This is a poem I wrote for the tragedies and injustice to the Aboriginal children.

(Published by Polar Expressions Publishing in a book Titled Behold)

It is now part of the national collection at Library and Archives in Ottawa for preservation in Canada's documentary history.

Under the earth lies tiny souls

A monstrous act, to the world untold

Remains are found, the numbers are high
Leaving in tears to cry

An injustice was carried

The precious unburied

Lies had been told
Their bodies were left cold.

Unimaginable to envision

A culture being poisoned

Your blood was shamed

A number was given, forgotten by name.

Unhuman and unremoved
These crimes were unrationed

In the devil's hands you were placed
To try and erase a beautiful human race.

Survivors were broken
Their innocence taken

Classmates, friends, and relatives found
Their bodies were hidden under the ground.

An unthinkable way

Words cannot say

How much we care

For the suffering you bear.

May justice prevail

May the innocent sail

May their souls rest in peace?

May they punish the beast?

Uniting together, standing up tall

Uniting together never to fall

Lighting a candle for all to see

Their angel wings finally set free.

Hold my hand

Let's dig in the sand

Rested properly

Remember the tragedy.

Believe in yourself

In a world made of stone

Where you have nowhere to call home

You search through each road

Hoping this one, will be gold

On this earth of judgment

Where there's jealousy and resentment

Turning on ourselves negatively

As we hold a perfect picture sturdy

As we glance or stare through the mirror
Our vision can alter the image greater

Criticizing ourselves with our mind and eyes

A cycle that destroys and lies

An angel and a demon at war

Knocking us right down to the floor

Abusing ourselves physically or mentally

In torment, we feel it melancholy

The opinion of those that could dig one's grave

Should come in and out, as quickly as saved

No human has the right to add to our dignity

Unless it is positive, they can keep their tragedy

Having faith in yourself can be empowering

Losing hope can be head-scratching

Nourish your soul with confidence

Be proud of all your accomplishments

Soar like an eagle in the starry night

Take wing, left and right

An amazing soul radiates in you

Look within, change your point of view

Amour propre, know thyself

Walk tall, believe in yourself

Made in the USA
Columbia, SC
15 April 2022

59052325R00113